THE WORLD
IN THE TIME OF
MARCO POLO

Chelsea House Publishers
Philadelphia

FIONA MACDONALD

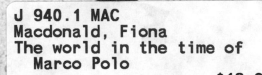

First published in hardback edition in 2001
by Chelsea House Publishers, a subsidiary of
Haights Cross Communications. All rights reserved.
Printed and bound in China.

First published in the UK in 1997 by
Belitha Press Limited, London House,
Great Eastern Wharf, Parkgate Road,
London SW11 4NQ, England

Text copyright © Belitha Press 1997
Text by Sarah McNeill & Fiona Macdonald
Map by John Fitzmaurice & Robin Carter

Editor: Claire Edwards
Design: Juanita Grout and Jamie Asher
Picture Researcher: Diana Morris
Consultant: Sallie Purkiss

First printing
1 3 5 7 9 8 6 4 2

The Chelsea House World Wide Web
address is: **http://www.chelseahouse.com**

Library of Congress Cataloging-in-Publication Data applied for.

ISBN: 0-7910-6033-0

Picture acknowledgments:

AKG, London: 3 Erich Lessing; 6tr, 7b Bibliothèque Nationale, Paris;
28b Erich Lessing; 32b Osterreichische Nationalbibliothek, Vienna;
44t Tretjakow Galerie, Moscow.
Bibliothèque Nationale, Paris: 33t.
Bridgeman Art Library: front cover c Giraudon/ Museo Correr, Venice;
1cr British Library, London; 6c, 7c San Marco, Venice; 12 Victoria & Albert
Museum, London; 15t British Library, London; 17t Bibliothèque Nationale,
Paris; 18 Private Collection; 19t Bibliothèque Nationale, Paris; 20t, 21b British
Library, London; 22t Bibliothèque Nationale, Paris; 28t British Library, London;
29t National Museum of American Art, Smithsonian Permlet Art Resource;
30t, 30b Private Collection; 32t British Library, London; 38t Victoria &
Albert Museum, London; 39t Bibliothèque Nationale, Paris; 40t Victoria
& Albert Museum, London; 42 Christies, London; 44b San Francesco
Upper Church, Assisi.
E.T. Archive: 1cl, 4 Bodleian Library, Oxford; 5; 6tl National Palace Museum,
Taiwan; 22c; 25t Freer Gallery of Art, Washington; 26b Bibliothèque Nationale,
Paris; 31b National Palace Museum, Taiwan; 41b Templo Mayor Museum,
Mexico City.

Picture acknowledgments cont:

Werner Forman Archive: 1cr Boston Museum of Fine Arts; 13t Beijing
Museum; 15b Canterbury Museum, Christchurch; 17b; 19b Boston Museum
of Fine Arts; 23t; 23b Private Collection; 27t; 29b Canterbury Museum,
Christchurch; 33b British Museum, London; 37b De Young Museum;
38b Courtesy Entwistle Gallery, London; 43b Private Collection, New York;
45t A.L. Larom Collection, Plains Indian Museum, Cody, Wyoming, USA.
Sonia Halliday Photographs: 14c Jane Taylor; 26t, 27b.
Robert Harding Picture Library: front cover, 16b, 20b British Museum, London;
24 Bibliothèque Nationale, Paris; 35b; 36 Gavin Hellier; 39b Adam Woolfit;
43tr M. Daniell; 45b Jennifer Reid.
Michael Holford Photographs: 2, 14b, 34, 40b.
Hutchison Picture Library: 21t Sarah Errington; 35t H.R. Dorig; 37t.
Royal Asiatic Society, London: 31t.
N.J. Saunders: 41t.
Zefa: 25b.

CONTENTS

ABOUT THIS BOOK

This book tells the story of Marco Polo and also looks at what was happening all around the world in his time. To help you find your way through the book, each chapter has been divided into seven sections. Each section describes a different part of the world and is headed by a color bar. As you look through a chapter, the color bars tell you which area you can read about in the text below. There is a time line, to give you an outline of world events in Marco Polo's time, and also a map, which shows some of the most important places mentioned in this book.

On page 46 is a list of some of the peoples you will learn about in this book. Some of the more unfamiliar words are also listed in the glossary.

THE STORY OF MARCO POLO

Marco Polo is one of the most famous people who lived in medieval Europe. He was an Italian merchant and explorer, who spent more than 20 years traveling around the world. This book tells you about some of his adventures, and about some of the people he met, the places he visited, and the wonderful sights he saw. It also tells you what was happening elsewhere in the world in Marco Polo's time, in countries he did not visit.

Marco Polo lived from 1254 until 1324, but this book covers a longer time span, from about 1200 to 1350. This will help you to find out about events that shaped the world before Marco Polo was born, and to discover what happened in the years soon after he died.

◄ The port of Venice, Marco Polo's hometown. Rich citizens stroll through the streets, while merchant ships unload valuable cargoes from faraway lands.

A FAMILY OF MERCHANTS

Marco Polo was born into a family of merchants. His father, Nicolo Polo, and his two uncles, Maffeo and Marco, all made money through buying and selling. The Polo family lived in Venice, a busy port and the biggest trading city in Italy. Merchants arrived there from many lands, loaded with exotic wares–jewels from India, gold from Africa, perfumes from Arabia, and silk and spices from the Far East.

BUYING AND SELLING ABROAD

Around 1250, one of Marco Polo's relatives left Venice to set up a business in the market city of Sudak, on the shores of the Black Sea. He traded with merchants from Central Asia, who sold goods they had carried long distances overland, from India and China. He bought these goods, took them home to Venice, and sold them in the markets there.

In 1260, Marco Polo's father and his uncle Maffeo had a bright idea. Rather than buying Eastern goods at high prices in Sudak, they would go to the Far East. There they could buy silks and jewels more cheaply and bring them back to Europe to sell. That way they would make more money.

Nicolo and Maffeo spent nine years traveling. They finally reached China, where they met the mighty ruler, Kublai Khan. He sent them back to Europe with a message for the Pope and invited them to visit China again.

MARCO'S JOURNEY BEGINS

In 1271 Nicolo and Maffeo Polo set off to visit China for a second time. This time young Marco went with them. He was only 17 years old. Their journey was nearly 15,000 miles long, and took them three and a half years. They traveled first by sea and then overland. They had to trek over high mountain passes and across treacherous deserts. They faced shipwrecks, pirates, and bandits. They suffered from sunstroke and frostbite, food poisoning, hunger, and thirst.

► Marco Polo, aged about 20. In his book, Marco boasted that he was a young man of "sound judgment and true worth."

▼ The map below shows the many places that Marco Polo visited on his travels between 1271 and 1295.

▼ Kublai Khan, Mongol emperor of China. Marco Polo described him in his book as the "mightiest man in the world."

▲ Precious stones from the Far East, polished and set in gold by craft workers in medieval Venice. Jewels like these were worth a fortune to merchants who brought them to Europe from distant lands.

IN CHINA

At last the Polos reached China and made their way to a place called Shangdu, in the wild countryside north of the present-day city of Beijing. Kublai Khan was staying there, and Nicolo and Maffeo were eager to meet him again and introduce him to young Marco.

Kublai greeted the Polos like old friends. They stayed in Kublai's wonderful palace, which was built of sparkling white marble, inlaid with gold. Close by there was a fantastic bamboo pavilion, decorated with dragons, where Kublai held huge feasts for up to 40,000 guests at a time. Marco reported that the weather at Shangdu was always fine while Kublai Khan was there, because he employed enchanters to make spells to drive the rain clouds away.

WORKING FOR THE EMPEROR

Kublai Khan was impressed by young Marco's intelligent appearance and offered him a job as a special investigator. He had to report anything suspicious he saw in the emperor's lands. For the next 17 years Marco traveled all over China. He also visited many other lands in the Far East, including India, Tibet, Burma (now Myanmar), and Vietnam. Everywhere he went, he watched what was going on—what people looked like, what they wore, and how they built their houses. He saw the foods they grew and how they made all kinds of goods, from big ships to delicate luxuries such as porcelain cups and silk cloth.

◄ Kublai Khan welcomes Marco Polo and his uncles to his summer palace at Shangdu. The palace was surrounded by fountains, streams, and beautiful gardens. Kublai stayed there every year to go hunting. Marco reported that Kublai had a specially trained leopard that rode beside him on his horse, then leaped off to chase and kill deer.

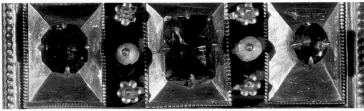

MARCO'S STORY

We know about Marco's travels because they were written down in a book. In 1298, when Venice was at war with Genoa, another Italian city, Marco Polo was captured and put in prison. While he was there, he met a famous writer called Rustichello of Pisa. To pass the time before they were set free, Marco told Rustichello what had happened on his travels, and Rustichello wrote it all down.

Marco's story became very popular. It was copied carefully by hand (because printing had not yet been invented in Europe) into many different languages. Because all Marco's stories seemed so spectacular, people thought he was exaggerating. He soon became known as Marco, the Million Man.

BACK TO ITALY

The Polos finally left China in 1292 and arrived home in Venice in 1295. By then their family and friends had given them up for dead and were suspicious of the three tired and dirty travelers in their shabby Chinese clothes. They didn't look at all like rich merchants. Then Marco, his father, and his uncle ripped open the secret pockets hidden inside their jackets, and heaps of precious jewels fell out. Everyone welcomed their return—and their riches—with a big feast and celebrations.

► The Polos sold the treasures they brought back from China to jewelers like these.

THE WORLD 1200–1350

ABOUT THE MAPS

The maps on this page will help you find your way around the world in Marco Polo's time. The big map shows some of the places and peoples mentioned in the text, including the following:

• **Towns**, **cities**, and **religious sites**. Some towns, such as Cuzco in South America, were rich in Marco Polo's time but are just roofless ruins today. Others, such as Khanbalik in northern China, have been replaced by modern cities with different names. (Khanbalik has been replaced by Beijing.)

• COUNTRIES that are different from modern ones. For example, the land Marco Polo called The Spice Islands today forms part of Indonesia.

• *Peoples*, such as the Aztecs. The descendants of these peoples often live in the same place today, but their traditional lifestyles have almost disappeared.

The little map shows the world divided into seven regions. The people who lived in a region were linked by customs, beliefs, or their environment. There were many differences within each region, but the people living there had more in common with each other than with people elsewhere. Each region is shown in a different color. The same colors are used in headings throughout the book to help you match the text with the region.

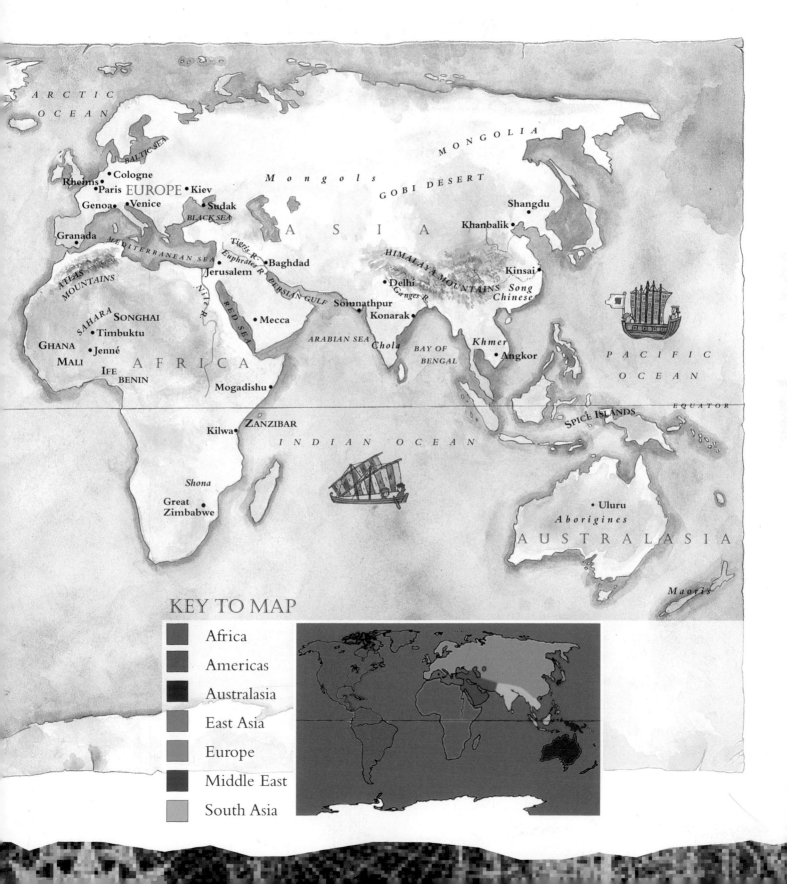

ARCTIC
OCEAN

BALTIC SEA

• Cologne
Rheims •
• Paris   EUROPE   • Kiev
Genoa •   • Venice   • Sudak
                    BLACK SEA

• Granada
        MEDITERRANEAN SEA

ATLAS
MOUNTAINS

MONGOLIA

M o n g o l s   GOBI DESERT

A S I A

• Shangdu

Khanbalik •

HIMALAYA MOUNTAINS

Tigris R.
Euphrates R.   • Baghdad
• Jerusalem   PERSIAN GULF

NILE R.

SAHARA   SONGHAI
        • Timbuktu
GHANA   • Jenné
MALI
    IFE
    BENIN

RED SEA

• Mecca

Somnathpur •

• Delhi
Ganges R.
        Konarak •

Chola

ARABIAN SEA

BAY OF
BENGAL

Kinsai •
Song
Chinese

Khmer
• Angkor

PACIFIC
OCEAN

A F R I C A

• Mogadishu

EQUATOR

SPICE ISLANDS

Kilwa •   • ZANZIBAR
        I N D I A N   O C E A N

Shona

Great
Zimbabwe •

• Uluru
Aborigines

A U S T R A L A S I A

Maoris

KEY TO MAP

	Africa
	Americas
	Australasia
	East Asia
	Europe
	Middle East
	South Asia

TIME LINE

1150   **1200**

EUROPE

1150–1350 Many universities built in northern Europe, including Paris (1150) and Oxford (1167).

1193 Indigo dye first imported to Britain from India.

1199 Richard the Lionhearted dies.

1175–1200 Italian scholars begin to translate scientific works by Middle Eastern scholars from Arabic to Latin.

1200–1350 Great age of cathedral and castle building.

c.1202 Use of Indian numbers spreads through Europe via Arabic translations. Now known as Arabic numbers.

1209 St. Francis of Assisi founds Franciscan brotherhood of friars.

1212 Children's Crusade.

1215 King John signs the Magna Carta in England

1226 Queen Blanche rules France (until 1235

1239 Mongols conquer Russia.

EAST ASIA

1159 Chinese make first-known printed map.

1192 Minamoto Yoritomo starts to rule Japan.

1193 Zen Buddhism introduced to Japan.

1206 Genghis Khan unites Mongol tribes.

1220 Mongols begin to advance toward Europe.

1221 Chinese design bombs containing shrapnel.

1232 Mongols use first-known rockets to attack Chinese.

1234 Mongols conquer northern China.

SOUTH ASIA

1100–1250 The Khmers build huge palace-temples, including Bayon.

1181 Jayavarman VII becomes last ruler of Khmer Empire.

1200–1300 Thai people leave China and settle in Thailand, which is still named after them.

1236 Raziya becomes first Muslim woman to rule in India (until 1240).

1206 Kingdom of Delhi established as independent state by Aibak.

MIDDLE EAST

1187 Saladin's army captures Jerusalem from the crusaders.

1193 Saladin dies.

c.1050–1250 Powerful Seljuk dynasty rules Eastern Turkey and many nearby lands.

1204 Crusaders capture Constantinople.

1218 Mongols conquer Iran.

AFRICA

c.1200 Cross-shaped churches built out of rock in Ethiopia.

c.1200 Great Mosque built at Kilwa.

c.1200–1300 East African trading ports grow rich as Indian Ocean trade increases.

1219 St. Francis of Assisi preaches in Egypt.

1235 Sundiata founds Empire of Mali, in West Afric

AMERICAS

c.1200 Chimu kingdom grows stronger along coast of northern Peru.

c.1200 Manco Capac becomes first Inca ruler. Founds Inca city of Cuzco, in Peru.

c.1200 Aztecs arrive in Mexico, probably from lands farther north.

AUSTRALASIA

c.1100–1300 New Zealand settlers move inland and build farms and villages, and grow crops.

c.1200–1300 Earliest-known rock paintings in New Zealand.

C. stands for *circa*, or about. It is used before dates that are approximate.

1250   **1300**   **1350**

1254 Marco Polo born.

1265 Dante Alighieri, Italian poet, born.

c.1267 Giotto, Italian painter and architect, born.

1267 English scientist Roger Bacon invents spectacles.

1271 Marco Polo begins his travels.

1272 Edward I becomes King of England.

1276 King Edward I of England invades Wales.

1280 Spinning wheel invented in Germany.

1295 First parliament meets in England.

1314–1320 Famine in Europe after harvests fail.

1314 Battle of Bannockburn. Scotland defeats England.

1324 Marco Polo dies.

1337 Hundred Years War begins between England and France (ends 1453).

1340 Chaucer, English poet, born.

1347 First outbreak of Black Death in Europe.

c. 1350 Guns first used in Europe.

1260 Kublai Khan becomes Mongol emperor (until 1294).

1276 Chinese astronomer Zhou Kung builds device to measure the shadow cast by the sun.

1279 Mongols conquer southern China.

1281 Mongol invasion of Japan fails.

1288 First-known gun made in China.

1327 Grand Canal completed in China.

1331 Outbreak of plague in northern China.

1336 Civil war in Japan between rivals wanting to be shogun.

1368 Mongols overthrown by Chinese.

c.1250 Chola Empire in southern India collapses. Land is divided into smaller, but still rich, states.

1287 Cambodia and Burma invaded by Mongols.

c.1250 Thai people conquer Khmer Empire.

c.1299 Mongols attack India, but mountains and climate force them to retreat.

1332 Outbreak of plague in India.

c.1250 Muslim doctors perform operations to cure blindness by removing cataracts.

1258 Mongols destroy Baghdad.

1259 Growth of Byzantine Empire as center of arts and learning.

1260 Mameluke army from Egypt stops Mongol advance toward the Holy Land.

1291 Last crusaders leave the Holy Land.

c.1300 Ottoman dynasty in Turkey begins to conquer nearby lands.

1320 Hafiz, Persian poet, born.

1350 Arabian scholar Al Farisi discovers how rainbows are formed.

c.1250 Building begins at Great Zimbabwe, East Africa.

1250 Mamelukes begin to rule in Egypt.

c.1300 Benin, West Africa, begins to grow powerful.

1312 Mansa Musa becomes ruler of Mali.

1325 Ibn Battuta begins his travels.

1350 Kingdom of Songhai, West Africa, conquers land from Mali.

1300–1350 West African city, Timbuktu, becomes center of learning and arts.

c.1250–1300 Anasazi people abandon Mesa Verde settlement, Colorado, because of drought.

c.1250 Mississippi Valley civilization declines.

c.1325 Aztecs found new capital city at Tenochtitlán.

c.1300 First huge statues built on Easter Island.

Marco Polo reported tales of a mysterious southern continent, which may have been Australia. Indonesian traders sailed there around 1450 to trade with Aborigines on the northern coast. They may have traveled there earlier, but no written records survive.

AROUND THE WORLD

Marco Polo lived at a time when the world was full of contrasts. In many countries, towns were growing and trade was booming. Rulers built castles and new cities, made new laws, encouraged scholarship, and paid for wonderful works of art.

But there were also terrible wars and battles. Toward the end of Marco Polo's life, there were reports of a deadly plague in India and the Far East. By the 1340s, it had spread westward, carried by traders traveling overland. The plague killed almost one third of the people in Europe. Today we remember it as the Black Death.

▲ Mongol horsemen were famous for their skill as riders. They could turn around in the saddle while their horses were galloping along and shoot arrows at enemies who were chasing them.

HEART OF AN EMPIRE

EAST ASIA

In Marco Polo's time, a quarter of the earth was ruled by one nation, the Mongols. Their empire was the largest there has ever been. At first the Mongols lived as nomads, roaming across the grassy plains north and west of China. But by Marco Polo's time, their terrifying armies controlled lands stretching from the Arctic Ocean to the Persian Gulf, and from Hungary to Korea.

A BRILLIANT CIVILIZATION

In the years before the Mongols became powerful, China was divided into two separate kingdoms, north and south. In 1234 Mongol armies captured northern China. Thousands, maybe millions, of Chinese people were killed or captured and forced to work as slaves. The Mongol invaders seized the northern Chinese capital city, drove out the people, and built their own new capital, Khanbalik, nearby.

The Mongols conquered southern China in 1279. Since 960 it had been ruled by the Song dynasty and was the home of the most advanced civilization in the world. Scientists had made important inventions and discoveries, merchants were rich, and scholars were very learned. Life for many Chinese people, especially in big towns like the one in the picture, was very comfortable. When Marco Polo visited south China's biggest city, Kinsai, he described it as "the finest and most splendid city on earth." The Mongols did not destroy southern China. They were pleased to add it to their empire, because it was rich and produced valuable goods and foods. So they taxed it heavily instead.

▲ This picture is a detail from a painting on silk. It shows a busy street in the city of Kaifeng, once the capital city of southern China.

▼ In 1281 the Mongols tried, but failed, to invade Japan. Here you can see Mongol ships being swept away in stormy weather. The Japanese called the storm *kamikaze*, which means "a wind from heaven."

RICH CITIES

Parts of South Asia, such as Cambodia and Burma were invaded by the Mongols in 1287. Many fine buildings and fertile farms were damaged or destroyed. India was luckier. It was protected by the high Himalaya Mountains. The powerful city of Delhi ruled large parts of northern India. Marco Polo listed all the goods sold there: gold, silver, silk, spices, brass, and coconuts, as well as the "best cotton cloth in the world." In southern India the magnificent Chola Empire, ruled by Hindu kings, was beginning to collapse after almost 500 years. Chola land, temples, and palaces were divided between two local dynasties, who set up smaller kingdoms of their own.

▲ The Qutb Minaret, part of a mosque in Delhi called the Might of Islam. It's almost 246 feet high, and was built by General Aibak, who conquered Delhi in 1192. A minaret is a tower from which Muslim worshipers are called to prayer.

► Muslim pilgrims are on their way to the holy city of Mecca, in Arabia.

THE FALL OF BAGHDAD

Muslim princes, called caliphs, ruled a vast and wealthy empire in the Middle East. They lived in the city of Baghdad, in present-day Iraq. For centuries the city had been a center of government, learning, and the arts. The caliphs sent governors to rule distant parts of the empire, collect taxes, and enforce Muslim law. They kept large armies to defend the empire from bandits and invaders, so that scholars, merchants, and pilgrims could travel safely on business and for pleasure. But in 1258 the Mongols attacked Baghdad and burned it to the ground. The caliphs' splendid city was destroyed.

◀ This picture is from a thirteenth-century manuscript. It shows fighting during the crusades. You can see Christian soldiers wearing chain mail, led by a bishop, who has a cross on his hat.

THE CRUSADES

For more than 150 years before Marco Polo's time, Christians and Muslims had been fighting wars known as the crusades. They began in 1095 when the Christian ruler of Greece and western Turkey asked the Pope for help against Muslim invaders. In reply, Pope Urban II called on all Christians in Europe, from kings to peasants, to fight the invaders, and then march on to the city of Jerusalem in the Holy Land. They wanted to overthrow the Muslim rulers and set up Christian kingdoms there. This was bound to cause trouble, because Jerusalem was a holy place to Muslim and Jewish people, as well as to Christians.

Armies of Christian crusaders captured Jerusalem in 1099, but the fighting went on. The Pope's message had whipped up religious feelings, and soldiers, peasants, and even children set off from all over Europe to carry out his command. In 1212 an army gathered that was made up entirely of children. But they never reached the Holy Land. Some died of hunger and disease. Others were kidnapped and sold as slaves. Muslim troops led by Saladin (see page 20) had recaptured Jerusalem in 1187, but the crusaders were not finally driven from the Holy Land until 1291.

FINDING NEW ISLANDS

The islands of Australasia were separated from one another—and from the rest of the world—by deep and stormy oceans. But for more than 1,000 years, people living there had risked the winds and the waves and sailed from their homes in Indonesia and nearby islands in search of better food supplies and new land. Over the years they reached many different groups of islands in the Pacific, including Fiji, Tonga, and, last of all, New Zealand, around A.D. 900.

At first, New Zealand settlers stayed close to the coast, but between 1100 and 1300, they began moving inland. They cut down trees and bushes to clear the ground and built farms and villages. They surrounded them with strong fences made of wood.

▶ A pendant decorated with a pattern of fish. It was made in New Zealand, but is based on an ancient design that settlers brought with them from their original home.

SOLDIER KINGS

AFRICA

In North Africa the ancient land of Egypt was ruled by Muslim soldiers called Mamelukes. These soldiers had been slaves recruited to fight in the crusades. But they were so successful, they soon took over the government. They governed the country well and made the police and law courts work better. Under their rule, Egypt grew rich.

BUSY PORTS

There were many great kingdoms in Africa, such as Mali, Songhai, Ghana, Benin, and Zimbabwe. All grew rich from selling gold and other valuable minerals such as copper and iron. These were carried overland to busy ports on the east coast, such as Mogadishu and Kilwa. Traders there also sold leather, leopard skins, ivory, and slaves to merchants from India, Arabia, and other Persian Gulf lands.

KINGS AND LORDS

EUROPE

According to medieval law, all the land in each country in Europe belonged to the king. He ruled with the help of lords and knights, who fought alongside him in battle and offered him advice on how to govern. He rewarded these loyal followers by giving them large pieces of land, called manors. At first, all the farmwork on the manors was done by ordinary men and women. In return, they were given their own plots of land, where they grew crops and raised animals for food. By Marco Polo's time, these arrangements were beginning to change. Ordinary people paid the lords money to rent their plots of land, and the lords used the money to pay for full-time laborers to work on their farms.

▶ A map of North Africa from a fourteenth-century atlas. The artist has shown a camel, an elephant, and a merchant wearing a headdress and scarf to protect his face from the Sahara sands. The band of yellow stones shows the Atlas Mountains.

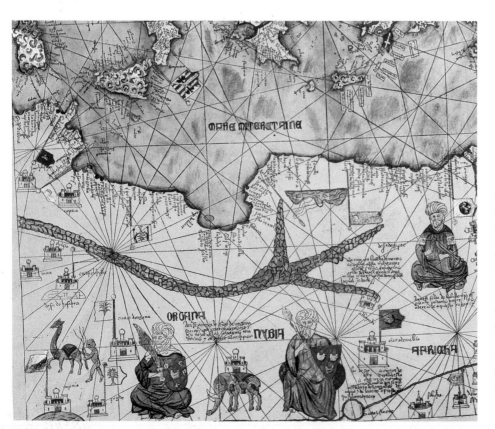

▶ Cliff Palace at Mesa Verde, Colorado. These multistory buildings were home to Native Americans known as the Anasazi from around 1100 to 1300. They were built of stone and sun-dried mud.

◄ A fair near Paris, France. The traders' stalls have canvas roofs. There is a stall for selling food and drink, and a shepherd with his sheep. In the center of the picture, a bishop is blessing the people who have come to the fair.

INTERNATIONAL TRADE

Throughout Europe the population was growing, land was cleared for farming, and new towns were built. Traders traveled long distances to sell their goods at markets and big international fairs. Industrial centers were also developing in Belgium and Italy. They made fine cloth from wool produced in England and Spain. In Germany and Poland there were busy ports on the shores of the Baltic Sea. The people there built ships, and sold tar, timber, furs, and salt fish.

MANY NATIONS

Many different groups of Native Americans were living in the Americas, including the nomad hunters of the Amazon rain forest, the farmers and traders of the Mississippi Valley, the Toltecs, who lived in hot, dusty Mexico, and the Incas in the Andes mountain valleys. Each group developed a lifestyle that helped its people survive in an often harsh environment. Each group also created spectacular buildings and amazing works of art.

Over the years native peoples changed. Some grew rich and powerful through trade, hunting and farming, or, sometimes, war. Others became weak because of famine and disease. A few, such as the Anasazi people of Mesa Verde, were forced to leave their homeland because the climate changed. The weather became hotter and drier, and all their crops failed.

FAMOUS RULERS AND LEADERS

In the past, millions of ordinary people, all over the world, lived and died without their names ever being written down. We know only about the lives of people who were famous, or who seemed important to the scribes. The scribes wrote mostly about powerful people, such as war leaders, kings, and queens. In this chapter you can read about some of the people who were famous in Marco Polo's time.

GENGHIS KHAN

EAST ASIA

Genghis Khan was born around 1162 in northeast Mongolia. When he was 13, his father was murdered by a rival. From then on Genghis had to fight to protect himself and his family. He fought with such skill that he soon became leader of his tribe. For the next 20 years, he fought many battles against rival tribesmen. Finally, in 1206, all the Mongol tribes agreed to obey Genghis as their leader. He was the first person ever to unite them. The Mongols now formed a terrifying army. They conquered all the neighboring lands, killing everyone who would not surrender. When Genghis died in 1227, his empire stretched from China to Turkey. He made strict laws, but his rule brought peace to conquered lands. Although he was cruel in battle, Genghis allowed the people in his empire to follow their own customs and religions.

▲ Mongol warriors fought on horseback. They rode very fast, day and night, to make surprise attacks on their enemies. They did not stop for food or rest, but drank sour milk from leather flasks and slept in the saddle as their horses galloped along.

KUBLAI KHAN

Kublai Khan, Genghis's grandson, ruled the
Mongol Empire from 1260 to 1294. He lived
most of his life in China, in the city of Khanbalik.
Kublai admired Chinese civilization, but never
forgot where he came from. He planted grass
from the Mongolian plains in his palace
courtyard to remind him of home. The Chinese
thought that Kublai was a tyrant and plotted to
be free of his rule. But visitors from Europe were
amazed at how efficiently he ran his empire and
at the richness of the lands he ruled. You can see
a picture of Kublai Khan on page 6.

THE GREAT SHOGUNS

Japan had been ruled by emperors since about
600 B.C. They were helped by warlords, who
carried out their commands. Each warlord had
an army of warriors called samurai, who pledged
loyalty to him. The most important warlord was
called a shogun. By Marco Polo's time, shoguns
ruled Japan on behalf of the emperors, who spent
all their lives shut away in the royal palace.

◀ Genghis Khan sits on silk
cushions in his richly decorated
tent. When he became leader of
the Mongols, he changed his name
from Temujin to Genghis Khan,
which means "universal ruler."

SULTANS OF DELHI

SOUTH ASIA

In Marco Polo's time
powerful rivals fought to control the kingdom
of Delhi, in India. According to legend, around
1190 the king, Prithvi Raj, fell in love with a
foreign princess. He helped her run away so that
she could marry him, but her father was furious
and declared war on Delhi. The fighting that
followed made the kingdom weak and easy to
attack. In 1192 an Afghan warrior, Qutb-ud-Din
Aibak, invaded Delhi, and Prithvi Raja was
killed. Aibak's family ruled Delhi for many years.
His granddaughter Raziya was the first Muslim
woman to rule in India, from 1236 to 1240.

▶ Minamoto Yoritomo
was a powerful shogun.
He ruled Japan from
1192 to 1199, and
founded a dynasty
of warrior rulers.
This picture
shows him ready
for war. Samurai
armor was made
of bamboo,
metal, and
leather.

SALADIN

Salah al–Din Yusuf ibn Ayyub was known in Europe as Saladin. He was one of the greatest war heroes of the crusades, and was still famous in Marco Polo's day. He lived from 1138 to 1193 and began his career as governor of Syria. Saladin led Muslim troops to many victories against Christian soldiers, who had invaded the Holy Land. In 1187 he captured the Holy City of Jerusalem from the Christians. King Richard the Lionhearted's English army failed to recapture it in 1189. The Christians never managed to win it back. But after a series of peace treaties in the thirteenth century, Marco Polo was able to visit Jerusalem safely in 1271.

◀ Saladin was a brilliant soldier and a wise ruler. This is the only known portrait of Saladin, but his secretary pictured him in words. He wrote that Saladin was "friendly, always kept his promises, and was loyal."

▲ Mansa Musa is shown here wearing a gold crown and holding a gold coin. His wealth came from Mali's gold fields, the richest in Africa at that time.

THE GOLDEN KING

In 1235 the empire of Mali, in West Africa, was founded by a warrior called Sundiata. He became the first mansa, or emperor, to rule its newly conquered lands. One of Mali's most magnificent rulers was Mansa Musa, who became emperor in 1312. He was famous as far away as Europe for his amazing wealth. He even had a channel built to bring river water to the desert, so that his wife could bathe in it.

Mansa Musa was a Muslim, and in 1324 he set off on a pilgrimage to the holy city of Mecca. He took with him 100 camels, each loaded with gold, and 60,000 servants. Wherever he stopped on a Friday, a holy day for Muslims, he gave the people who lived there enough money to build a mosque. He gave away so much on his pilgrimage that he had to borrow money from an Egyptian merchant to pay for his journey home.

GREAT CIVILIZATIONS

Mansa Musa was not the only African king to spend large sums of money on religious buildings and works of art. In Ethiopia the Christian rulers paid for splendid cross-shaped churches to be carved out of solid rock.

Oba Oguola ruled the kingdom of Benin from 1280 to 1295. During his reign, and that of the kings after him, craft workers produced lifelike bronze castings. Many were portraits of famous kings and queens. The cities of Benin were also rebuilt with fine palaces and trading houses.

▲ This church was built around 1200 for Ethiopian kings. The building is hollowed out of the rocky mountainside. The top of the roof is level with the ground.

TWO FAMOUS KINGS

EUROPE

Medieval people expected their kings to be bold, sometimes bloodthirsty, fighters. It was a king's duty to defend his kingdom and, if possible, to conquer new land. In Marco Polo's day many people admired two English kings: Richard I (called the Lionhearted), who died in 1199, and Edward I, who ruled from 1272 to 1307. Both were praised for their courage and leadership in battle.

In other ways, too, they were models of what medieval people thought kings and knights should be. Both were tall and handsome. Richard was a fine musician, and Edward was good at sports. Richard fought in the crusades against Saladin and his Muslim soldiers. Edward led the English army to conquer Wales and built eight magnificent castles there. He died of a fever while he and his troops were trying to conquer Scotland.

◄ King Edward I with some of his advisors. Young scribes, making notes, are crouching at his feet.

▲ Queen Blanche kneeling next to her husband, the King of France, at their wedding. All the most important people in France attended royal weddings, which were magnificent occasions.

▶ The Toltec god-king, Quetzalcoatl. The first Aztec leaders were said to be descended from him.

QUEEN BLANCHE AND SAINT LOUIS

EUROPE

Not all European rulers were warlike. Queen Blanche was scholarly, clever, and practical. There were very few women rulers in the Middle Ages, because most people thought that women were too weak to rule. But Blanche proved them wrong. She governed France successfully from 1226 to 1235, until her son, King Louis IX, was old enough to rule, and later during his absence on the crusades. Louis grew up to be very religious and gave rich treasures to the Church. He died while leading a crusade to the Holy Land. After his death church leaders made him a saint.

KING JOHN

A few European rulers became famous for their troubles. King John of England, the younger brother of Richard the Lionhearted, ruled from 1199 to 1216. He quarreled with the Church, fought his nephew (who had more right to be king), was defeated in a war with France, and ruled so harshly that the nobles of England threatened to rebel. In 1215 they made him promise to rule according to the law. This promise was written down in a document called the Magna Carta, which means Great Charter.

AZTECS

AMERICAS

In about 1200 the Aztec people arrived in Mexico from the north and founded a new kingdom. We do not know the names of their first rulers, but Toltec and Aztec legends told of a god-king called Quetzalcoatl. His name meant "feathered serpent." The picture above comes from an Aztec codex. These books told the stories of Aztec gods and leaders in brightly colored pictures.

▲ This totem pole was carved from a single tree trunk. Totem poles recorded family history and important events. They often pictured myths and legends, too.

STORIES IN ART

There were many powerful people living in North America in Marco Polo's time—great hunters, war leaders, wise women, and chiefs. But we do not know their names because the Native Americans did not use writing. Instead, they relied on memory or works of art to record their past. Craft workers painted picture histories, or carved totem poles to mark important events. Native American people also told exciting stories about heroes and heroines, such as Kaletaka, a magical warrior figure honored by the Hopi Native people of Arizona. Some of these stories must have been based on real people, who had lived and been famous long ago.

BRAVE CHIEFS

There are no written records from Australasia to tell us famous people's names. But we can tell from the buildings and works of art that survive that rich, powerful people lived in these lands. Craft workers built great memorials, like the Ha'amonga-a-Maui (coral archway) in Tonga, in honor of brave chiefs and their sons. People also praised sailors and explorers in stories and songs.

LEADERS AND LEGENDS

In South America the names of a few famous people have survived in stories and legends. But we do not know for certain whether they existed. Legends from Peru tell the story of Manco Capac and his sister, Mama Ocilo, who became the first rulers of the new Inca nation around 1200. Manco was told by the sun god to look for a new land. The sun god gave him a golden rod and told him to throw it down on the ground as he searched. If the ground swallowed it up, he should build a city there. The city he finally founded was called Cuzco.

► A stone carving from Australia, made to keep alive the memory of ancient ancestors.

HOW PEOPLE LIVED

▼ Camels carry boxes of salt and bags of gold across the Sahara. In Marco Polo's time, long-distance travel was often dangerous and always very slow. It could take three months to cross the Sahara.

If you could travel back to Marco Polo's time, you would find that peoples' lives were very different from today. There were only a few big cities and towns. Most ordinary people lived in the country and worked on the land. Their houses were small and were made of local materials, such as wood, mud, and thatch. They had no gas or electricity and no fresh water on tap. Their food was plain and simple, and their clothes were rough and homemade. On the following pages, you can see some of the many different peoples and lifestyles Marco Polo described in his book. You can also find out about life in countries that he never visited, and in lands such as America and Australia, which he did not know even existed.

◄ In the foreground of the picture, a Chinese farmworker carries two big straw baskets of rice. A government official, dressed in a fine silk robe, looks on. The workers wear rough jackets and trousers.

A HARSH LAND

Unlike China, the Mongols' homeland was barren. Few crops would grow there, so the Mongols raised herds of oxen, horses, and goats. They were suspicious of vegetables, which they thought made people weak. Their main foods were meat and milk, with a few wild herbs and onions. Rich Mongols enjoyed hunting and eating bears and deer. But ordinary Mongol families ate any meat they could catch, even rats and mice. In emergencies they made a cut in a horse's vein and drank the blood.

COUNTRY AND TOWN LIFE

EAST ASIA

In the picture above, you can see Chinese farmworkers busy at harvest time. People's lives depended on a good harvest–if crops failed, they would starve. Rice was the main crop in southern China, but wheat and millet grew better in the north. Chinese farmers also kept tea gardens, vegetable plots, fish farms, and orchards, and raised pigs, chickens, and ducks. Chinese villages were often surrounded by a strong wall for protection against bandits and thieves.

China was rich and had a rapidly growing population, so some people left the country to live in towns. They hoped to make their fortunes by working as craft workers, merchants, or government officials. To feed them and their families, farm produce was carried to the towns every day by riverboat and ox cart. Marco Polo enjoyed tasting the rice wine and yellow peaches that he found on sale in town markets.

► A campsite in modern-day Mongolia. Each family has its own tent. The Mongol lifestyle that Marco Polo described still survives today.

A NOMADIC LIFESTYLE

To feed their animals, the Mongols had to follow a nomadic way of life. They moved from one place to another, seeking fresh grass. They lived in big felt tents, called yurts, which could be packed up and moved around. Mongol men and women kept warm by wearing long fur-lined coats and woolen shirts, with leather trousers and thick boots.

THE SPICE ISLANDS

Sweet-smelling spices, such as cloves, nutmeg, and pepper, were highly valued in Europe and the Middle East for use in medicines, as perfumes, and for flavoring food. But spices grew in places like South Asia, which had a hot, damp climate all year. They grew best in the Spice Islands, now the Moluccas, part of Indonesia. People living there became rich by selling spices to merchants from distant lands. They also used spices to flavor their own local foods, including coconuts, rice, milk, fish, and fruit.

RIVERSIDE FARMS

Much of the Middle East was desert, but two great rivers, the Tigris and the Euphrates, flowed through Iraq. Farmers there dug irrigation channels to carry river water to their fields, then planted crops of wheat, melons, eggplants, and sugar cane in the rich, muddy soil. On drier land they planted orchards of apricot and almond trees, and date palms for their sweet sticky fruit. They kept sheep and goats to provide them with wool, leather, meat, and milk. Marco Polo especially liked a drink he tasted here, made from dates and spices.

▲ Iraqi farmers planted crops in irrigated fields. Like farmers all over the world, they had no machines to help them. They relied on the muscle power of animals and people.

◄ This picture shows a European merchant bargaining with pepper growers in India. Indian merchants also sold fine cotton cloth, like the loincloths the workers are wearing.

BUSY TOWNS

The picture on the opposite page shows two wealthy travelers arriving in a small market town. Many Middle Eastern towns would have looked like this. Their busy streets had mosques, bazaars, drinking-water fountains (essential in a hot, dry land), drugstores, craft studios, and public baths. There might be hospitals, libraries, and schools, and also inns, called khans, where traveling merchants could stay.

Rich townspeople lived in very comfortable homes. Their houses were built around a courtyard, which was cool in summer, and had thick walls for privacy and warmth. Inside there were beautiful carpets, silverware, pottery, and glass. Ordinary people lived in smaller, one-roomed houses, made of mud brick.

▲ The ruins of Great Zimbabwe. *Zimbabwe* means "important stone houses" in the Shona language. About 18,000 people lived there, safe behind stone walls.

▼ These Syrian travelers are wearing cloaks and turbans of brightly colored silk. Behind them, the townspeople are busy working in their homes.

DESERT GOLD

In the hot Sahara of North Africa, nomads lived in tents and raised herds of camels. They sold these to traders making the long journey south across the Sahara. South of the desert, in trading towns like Jenné and Timbuktu, Middle Eastern merchants swapped salt from the northern Sahara and cloth from Syria and Iran for African produce such as gold, sandalwood, and animal skins. Some merchants also bought slaves.

CATTLE AND IRON

Some East African peoples lived as nomads, herding cattle and hunting elephants for ivory and leopards for their skins. Others, such as the Shona people, settled in village houses made of timber and mud. They grew crops of millet and beans and mined gold, copper, and iron. They bartered these for Chinese pottery, Middle Eastern glass, and jewelry with merchants who traded at ports along the east coast. By around 1250 the Shona were rich enough to build a city at Great Zimbabwe. It was a trading center, and a home for their kings.

LIVING FROM THE LAND

EUROPE

In northern Europe, farming was hard work all year round. In lowland areas villagers grew wheat, barley, and oats in big open fields. Men plowed, women weeded, and children scared birds away. Everyone helped at harvest time. Lowland farmers also tended orchards and vineyards, to produce apples, grapes, cider, and wine. Women grew cabbages, leeks, garlic, and herbs in cottage gardens, raised chickens and pigs, and kept bees. Rich people ate the best of this food: roast meat, honey sweets, and spiced wine. Ordinary people ate black bread, cheese, and vegetable soup.

▲ At harvest, women and girls cut the ripe wheat with sharp curved knives, called sickles, while men gathered the wheat into bundles to dry in the sun.

MOUNTAIN LIFE

In mountain regions, people lived by hunting and by gathering wild foods, such as mushrooms, nuts, and berries. In the summer they grazed cows, sheep, and goats on mountain meadows and used the milk to make cheese. They traded this for lowland grain at market towns or country fairs.

▶ A street in a town in Italy. In the foreground of the picture, there is a tailor's shop. All clothes were sewn by hand, but only rich people could afford to buy fine clothes from shops like these.

TRADE AND TOWNS

In Italy, Spain, and southern France, there were many thriving towns. People living there made their money from craft work or by buying and selling goods in shops or at the market. Town life was busy and interesting, but towns could be very crowded. Town-dwellers had to put up with noisy neighbors, burglars, and beggars, plus smells and diseases caused by open sewers in the middle of many town streets. With so many kitchens, taverns, and workshops, there was also a constant risk of fire.

Ordinary town houses were made of wood, plaster, or brick, but the finest homes, like the ones below, were made of stone. They were tall and built close together, to make the best use of valuable space within the safety of the town's strong walls. Merchants often used the ground-floor rooms of their homes as shops. They could afford big houses and beautiful furniture, but the poor lived in single rooms and slept on straw.

CITIES AND TOWNS

Native American peoples in different natural environments lived in very different ways. Some lived in large, well-planned cities and towns. The city of Cahokia, in the Mississippi Valley, was home to more than 10,000 people. They lived by trade and by growing corn on the surrounding land. In Arizona, people lived in villages called pueblos. Each pueblo contained dozens of houses made of sun-dried brick, joined together like modern apartment buildings.

NOMAD LIVES

Many Native Americans were nomads. On the Great Plains, they lived in tents called tepees and hunted the vast herds of buffalo that roamed there. Other American peoples were nomads, too. In winter, in the Arctic, Thule and Inuit hunters lived in igloos made of blocks of snow. They speared seals, whales, and walruses through the ice for food and skins. They also used the bones for making weapons. In summer they camped in skin tents. They fished from skin-covered canoes and hunted reindeer, called caribou.

MEAT AND BERRIES

The Aborigines of Australia lived in small groups. They moved from camp to camp, collecting seeds and berries, digging for roots, and hunting kangaroos. They also caught fish and trapped eels and waterbirds. In summer they usually wore nothing at all, or just a loincloth. In winter they wore cloaks made of opposum skins. For shelter they made huts of branches and twigs.

▲ Native American hunters disguised in wolf skins creep close to a herd of buffalo. They attacked the weakest of the herd with bows and arrows and spears.

FISH AND FEATHERS

In Polynesia, people caught fish and shellfish, dug for yams, and collected coconuts. They made houses from wood and thatched the roofs with coconut leaves. Women wove skirts out of grass. In New Zealand, settlers cut down trees, built villages, and planted fields of sweet potatoes. They made cloaks of feathers plucked from kiwis to keep themselves warm.

▼ A Maori rock drawing of two fishermen. The canoe is made of rushes and was used for fishing and hunting birds on lakes. On the right is a moa—a big, flightless bird that is now extinct.

DISCOVERY AND INVENTION

We might think that people in Marco Polo's time lived very simple lives, because they had few machines or tools to help them. In fact, there were many skillful medieval scientists, engineers, and inventors, though they often combined new ideas with traditional beliefs. Because some countries did not keep written records, we do not know exactly when many inventions and discoveries were first made, although we can tell from books like Marco Polo's when some inventions became widely used.

In Marco Polo's time, few people could read or write, and long-distance travel was very slow. This meant that news spread slowly, too. Sometimes, people in distant countries invented similar things at different times. For example, printing with movable type was invented in China around 1050, then separately, in Europe, around 1450.

► Chinese craft workers printed paper money, like this banknote from Kublai Khan's reign. Paper was easier to carry around than silver or gold, and less likely to be stolen. Paper money was not used in Europe until the seventeenth century.

▼ Traditional Indian stories tell how a famous poet and singer called Amir Khusrau invented the sitar, a musical instrument, in the early fourteenth century. Sitar players composed special tunes to fit in with the season of the year or the time of day.

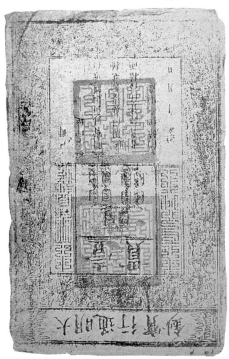

▲ Indian cloth workers printed fabric by dipping a block of wood carved with a pattern into a bowl of liquid dye, then pressing it onto plain cloth.

GREAT INVENTORS

EAST ASIA

Marco's book is full of admiring descriptions of Chinese inventions and discoveries. Many had been invented hundreds of years before, but were still unheard of in Europe. The Chinese had silk, paper money, mechanical clocks, wheelbarrows, magnetic compasses, and kites. They had also invented guns, rockets, and instruments to measure the movements of stars and planets. The Mongol conquerors of China continued to develop this technology. Kublai Khan commissioned great engineering projects, including paved roads, bridges, and the Grand Canal, which was completed in 1327. The canal linked the capital city with farms and trading towns over 1,100 miles away.

Marco was also impressed by Kublai Khan's postal service, which kept the emperor in touch with the far corners of his empire at a time when there was no radio, television, or telephone. Relays of messengers ran day and night, passing on the message from person to person. They covered in 24 hours the distance that took other travelers ten days.

WONDERFUL NUMBERS

SOUTH ASIA

India was famous for its mathematicians. Around 200 B.C. they had invented the idea of the zero, along with the system of numbers, called Arabic numerals, used worldwide today. These numbers spread to Europe in Marco Polo's time, reaching England around 1400. They replaced the old European use of Roman numerals to write numbers (I, II, III, etc.). Indian numbers made all kinds of calculations much easier for merchants, tax collectors, bankers, and scientists.

COLORS FOR CLOTH

Indian craft workers were expert at weaving fine white cotton cloth, but they were less successful at coloring it. So they experimented to invent new kinds of dyes. They mixed plants, metals, and powdered earth and produced strong, rich colors. Around 1200 they discovered how to make a deep blue dye from the indigo plant. It is still used to dye cloth, including that for jeans.

▼ A bridge in the busy city of Kaifeng, once capital of south China. Marco Polo was impressed by the huge and beautiful bridges he saw in many Chinese cities.

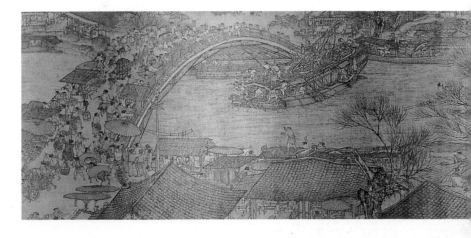

SUN AND STARS

MIDDLE EAST

Muslim scientists were famous for their achievements. They were the first to make magnifying lenses, around 1050. (In 1260, an Englishman called Roger Bacon used this technology to invent the first pair of spectacles.) Muslim astronomers also invented instruments to help them observe the sun, moon, and stars. One of these, the astrolabe, measured the height of the sun in the sky. It was used by sailors to work out their position at sea.

MUSLIM MEDICINE

In the Middle East and Europe, there were many ideas about what caused disease. Some people trusted in homemade herbal cures. Others prayed for good health and went on pilgrimages. Some scholars believed health was linked with the movements of the moon and planets. But most doctors in the Middle East relied on more scientific treatments. They studied how the body worked (sometimes by cutting up dead bodies), noted their patients' state of mind and lifestyle, and made records of which medicines made a patient better or worse. There were doctors and pharmacists in many Middle Eastern towns, and the first hospitals were built there. But compared with modern times, many more patients died.

► Opposite is a picture of an Arabian dhow. You can see an anchor at the prow (front) and a rudder at the stern (back).

◄ Muslim astronomers with their books and scientific instruments. One of them is holding an astrolabe (the big gold-colored disk).

GREAT ENGINEERS

Some of the best Muslim technology was designed for war, or to help people survive in a harsh environment. Scientists made machines to smash holes in castle walls and invented new weapons, such as naphtha. This was a burning mixture that could not be put out with water. In 1172, General Nur al-Din, governor of Syria and Egypt, had the bright idea of using homing pigeons to send and receive messages from spies and army commanders in enemy lands. It helped him win many battles during the crusades.

More peacefully, engineers in Syria designed huge wheels to lift water to fields from deep river beds. They dug underground channels to let melted snow flow from mountains to low-lying desert lands, for drinking and to irrigate crops. Architects designed wind funnels, like chimneys, to bring cooling breezes into hot city homes.

◄ A Muslim doctor at work. Doctors treated patients with special foods, and drugs made from all kinds of herbs.

METALWORKING

In Marco Polo's time, African craft workers were perfecting metalworking techniques using gold, silver, iron, and bronze. Ibn Battuta wrote about the skilled ironworkers who lived on the coast of East Africa. Others were working inland, in Zimbabwe.

In West Africa, metalworkers in the kingdoms of Ife and Benin used the lost-wax process to produce beautifully detailed sculptures, like the head below. First they made a solid head out of mud. Then they covered it in wax, on which they molded the fine detail. This was coated with more layers of mud and then burned in a bonfire, until the wax melted and ran out through holes in the mud. Hot liquid bronze was poured into the gap left by the wax. Once the metal had cooled, the outer layers of mud were chipped off, and the inner core of mud dug out. This left a hollow, lifelike bronze head.

STEERING SHIPS

Middle Eastern merchants sailed down the Persian Gulf and across the Indian Ocean to buy spices and other valuable goods in India and beyond. Their ships were called dhows. They were made of planks of wood, sewn together with rope, and fitted with rudders at the back. Rudders were a Chinese invention that Muslim sailors copied some time after 100 A.D. They made ships much easier to steer.

IBN BATTUTA

AFRICA

Marco Polo was not the only explorer of his time. Ibn Battuta was born in Tangier, North Africa, in 1304. When he was 21, he set off on a pilgrimage to the Muslim holy city of Mecca, then decided to continue his journey and explore the world. Ibn Battuta traveled across the Sahara with African merchants and visited many countries, including India, China, Spain, Turkey, and the Holy Land. When at last he returned home, he dictated his memoirs to a scribe. His descriptions of faraway lands became very popular, as well as useful to travelers, merchants, scientists, and geographers. In Africa and the Middle East, he was known as the Traveler of his Age.

▼ A bronze head of a king from Ife, in present-day Nigeria. It was made, probably in the thirteenth century, using the lost-wax process.

BUILDING CASTLES

EUROPE

In medieval Europe there were many builders and architects. Their biggest projects were castles and churches, which showed amazing technical and artistic skill. The first simple castles were built in the eleventh century, but over the next 200 years, designs were improved and became more complicated.

Castle design was a matter of life and death. If castles were not strong enough to survive an enemy attack, then the people inside would die. Some of the finest castles were built during the thirteenth century. Many special features gave the castles built then their extra strength. Choosing a good site was very important. The ideal position was on a tall cliff, or by the sea, so the castle could not be surrounded. Layout was also important. Thirteenth-century castles had a massive central tower, called a keep, with enormously thick walls made of pounded earth and rubble encased in solid stone.

▲ Conway Castle in Wales was built to guard King Edward I of England's newly conquered lands. Kings paid vast sums of money to get the best architects and engineers to design their castles.

The keep was surrounded by rings of outer walls, called curtain walls, and a deep ditch, called a moat. Each wall had lookout towers and a fortified gatehouse, with a drawbridge, a portcullis, and an iron-studded wooden door for extra defense. Even if attackers smashed their way through one outer wall, they still could not reach the lord and his knights sheltering in the keep. Keeps and towers were round, not square. This made it harder for attackers to dig underneath the walls and collapse them. Towers and keeps had narrow slit windows, so attackers could not climb in, which were topped with walkways called battlements. These were protected by walls with gaps at intervals, so that defenders could shoot down at the enemy.

◄ A rope bridge in the Andes Mountains. The Incas plaited reeds and twisted them into ropes to make fragile bridges. These rocked and swayed hundreds of feet above the valley floor below.

INCA BRIDGES

Native Americans invented many ways of traveling long distances quickly, carrying heavy loads. In the Andes the Incas developed a backpack supported by a broad strip of cloth, called a tumpline. It stretched across peoples' foreheads and shoulders. They could carry large bundles this way, and still have their hands free to help them scramble over rocky slopes. The Incas also made amazing rope bridges across mountain valleys. Bridges speeded journey times by letting travelers take the shortest and most direct route.

SURVIVAL ON LAND AND SEA

In Australia, Aborigines used their knowledge to help them track animals, catch fish, and find water. They invented tools, such as the boomerang, to help them hunt.

In the Pacific, people sailed in canoes with a special frame outside the boat called an outrigger. This made the canoe more stable in dangerous waves. Both the boomerang and the outrigger were unknown anywhere else in the world. Polynesian sailors also discovered how to find their way over vast unmapped oceans by observing the winds, waves, and stars.

TEPEE SLEDGE

AMERICAS

There were no horses in the Americas because the native American breed had died out thousands of years before Marco Polo's time. And although the Aztecs of Mexico made toys with wheels for their children to play with, there was no wheeled transportation anywhere in America.

In North America the nomadic peoples of the Great Plains invented a triangular sledge called a travois, made with tepee poles. When the time came to move camp, the travois was loaded with the tepee cover and all the tepee contents, then pulled along by women or dogs. The poles fanned out behind, spreading the load.

► A boomerang is a thin strip of wood that spins when it is thrown, so that it hits its target with greater force than a rock or a simple stick. Because it flies along a curved path, it also returns to the thrower.

THE CREATIVE WORLD

Many of the finest buildings and works of art in Marco Polo's time were created for religious purposes. Temples, mosques, and cathedrals encouraged everyone to worship God. But because they were often paid for by nobles, kings, and princes, they also reminded people of their ruler's wealth and power. Craft workers used traditional designs and techniques, and different styles developed around the world. Because travel and transportation were slow and expensive, artists and craft workers depended on local materials, such as clay, wood, and stone. They made dyes from plants, and paint from colored earth.

STATUES AND SCREENS

EAST ASIA

In Japan, sculptors produced calm images of the Buddha and lifelike statues of Buddhist monks and priests. Japanese painters created dramatic pictures on long scrolls, telling the story of battles between warlords and samurai armies. Warlords began building bigger and better castles, full of fine furniture and decorated with painted screens.

◄ This statue of Buddha comes from Tokyo, Japan. It was carved in the late thirteenth century.

FINE PORCELAIN

Fine Chinese porcelain was prized in East Africa, Asia, and the Middle East. Marco Polo saw mounds of special Chinese clay, dug up from underground and left in heaps to "ripen" for 40 years. This clay was shaped by potters into lovely dishes and bowls. It was then fired at very high temperatures in special ovens called kilns. Finally, it was covered with a delicate colored glaze and fired again. You can see some Chinese porcelain in the picture of Genghis Khan on page 19.

WONDERUL TEMPLES

SOUTH ASIA

In 1268, a star-shaped Hindu temple was built in the Indian city of Somnathpur. Around the same time another temple, shaped like the chariot that carried the Hindu sun god across the sky, was built at Konarak in north India. It had 12 carved stone wheels, and seven huge stone horses standing nearby. Indian sculptors decorated all their temples with carvings and statues of beautiful goddesses and powerful gods.

SHRINES AND KINGS

In Cambodia, wealthy Hindu and Buddhist kings built temple-palaces where they lived and were buried. One of the most beautiful was the temple of Bayon, built for Jayavarman VII. It had a golden tower surrounded by more than 20 stone towers. Each had four massive faces carved on it, believed to be of the king. Inside, the walls were covered in carvings showing battle scenes and royal life.

▲ Jayavarman VII ruled the Khmer Empire in Cambodia from 1181 to 1218. His face is carved in stone on the towers of the Bayon temple-palace in the city of Angkor.

PATTERNS AND WRITING

MIDDLE EAST

Many Muslim artists believed it was wrong to paint pictures or carve statues of living things, because only God had the power to create life. Instead, they painted and carved beautiful patterns, like the ones at the top of page 38. They also used special handwriting, called calligraphy, to write holy books and to decorate mosques, colleges, and tombs.

◀ Ganesha, the Hindu elephant-headed god of good fortune, carved in southern India, around 1200.

► Tiles with geometric patterns and Arabic calligraphy, such as this one, were used to decorate mosques and palaces in Muslim countries.

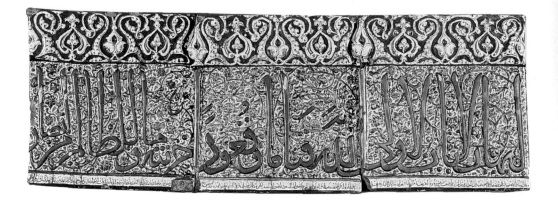

TILES AND CERAMICS

MIDDLE EAST

Middle Eastern craft workers made pottery, carpets, silk, metalwork, and glass. Marco Polo saw and admired all these on his travels. They also made patterned tiles to decorate important buildings. Tiles were made in flat, geometric-shaped molds, and painted with colored glazes that turned glassy when heated. They were attached to walls and floors in complicated designs.

PALACES, MOSQUES, AND TOMBS

AFRICA

On the coast at Kilwa, massive palaces were built of coral and carved with decorative patterns and designs. Remains found at Great Zimbabwe also show how rich the rulers of East Africa were. Palace rooms were full of gold ornaments, soapstone carvings, and dishes decorated with wild-animal designs of zebras, dogs, and baboons.

In West Africa, King Mansa Musa paid for two beautiful mosques to be built in the cities of Jenné and Timbuktu. They were made of clay, plastered over a framework of branches, in traditional local style. West African artists also made lifesize clay figures, like the horseman shown on this page. These statues were buried with kings and wealthy people in their tombs, to serve them after death.

◄ This figure of a warrior on horseback is from a tomb near Jenné, in Mali. It is made from baked clay, called terra cotta. The rider is wearing a necklace, and the horse has a decorated headdress.

NEW CATHEDRALS

If Marco Polo had traveled north to France and Germany, he would have seen some of Europe's greatest cathedrals being built, at Chartres, Paris, Rheims, and Cologne. They were designed by architects in the latest gothic style. They had huge windows with pointed arches, soaring roofs, and tall, slim spires. Only the most skilled craft workers, with years of training, were employed to build cathedrals. People wanted the very best for these houses of prayer.

LIFELIKE PICTURES

In Marco Polo's time Italian artists were beginning to develop a new, more realistic style of painting to decorate churches and cathedrals. The figures and scenery they painted were so lifelike that worshipers felt they had stepped into another world. There is a painting in this style by Giotto, of St. Francis, on page 44.

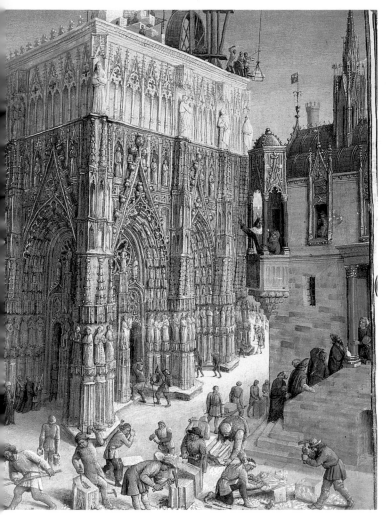

▲ Building a cathedral. At the front of the picture, masons are carefully shaping blocks of stone.

▼ A courtyard of a palace on the grounds of the Alhambra. The gardens and courtyards were full of fountains, pools, and plants.

MUSLIM SPAIN

EUROPE

Southern Spain was ruled by Muslim princes. But Muslims, Christians, and Jews lived side by side in a multicultural community. This is reflected in their art, which combines many different styles. Christian and Muslim craftsmen worked together to construct many fine buildings, including the Alhambra. This was a fortified palace, rebuilt during the fourteenth century for the rulers of Granada, in southern Spain. It is still one of the most beautiful buildings in the world.

▲ Small pieces of clear and colored glass were joined with strips of lead to make huge windows like these.

BEAUTIFUL BOOKS

EUROPE

Monks and nuns were some of the few people in Marco Polo's time who could read and write. They copied books by hand and decorated them with sheets of gold leaf and brilliant colors—some made of crushed semi-precious stones. The gold and bright colors made light seem to shine from the pages.

It could take a whole year for a monk to make one copy of the Bible. Sometimes the illustrations in medieval books and manuscripts were religious. Sometimes they showed ordinary people working and playing. These tiny pictures are one of our best sources of information about life in Marco Polo's time. You can see an example on page 28.

BRILLIANT GLASS

Churches and cathedrals were often decorated with windows made of stained (colored) glass. They glowed like rainbows, as the sun streamed through. Stained-glass windows often showed scenes from Bible stories. Ordinary people couldn't read, but they could look at the windows and learn from the pictures there.

GOLDEN MASKS

AMERICAS

In South America the Chimu people of Peru made precious objects out of pure, beaten gold. They made funeral masks to cover the faces of important dead people, and knives and dishes to use in religious ceremonies. The Chimu also made many beautiful objects out of mother-of-pearl.

◄ A Chimu gold knife, made in the shape of the god of the moon. It is decorated with turquoise beads.

STONE SKULLS

Between 900 and 1200, in big cities such as Chichén Itzá, the Maya people of Mexico built enormous temples on top of tall pyramid mounds. They were built as high as possible to reach up to the gods. Each temple was guarded by huge stone figures and decorated with rows of carved human skulls. These carvings recorded the human sacrifices that took place at the top of the temple steps.

▲ These mysterious statues were carved on Easter Island between about 1200 and 1500.

◄ An Aztec stone carving of an eagle knight. The knights wore special uniforms made of real eagle beaks and feathers.

EAGLE KNIGHTS

The Maya, and the Aztecs who lived in Mexico after them, carved statues of their bravest warriors, the fearsome eagle knights. Aztec artists cut rough blocks of stone with flakes of obsidian, which is a hard, glassy rock produced when volcanoes erupt. They then smoothed and polished their carvings with wet sand to add all the details of clothes, faces, and expressions.

EASTER ISLAND MYSTERY

On remote Easter Island in the South Pacific, artists carved about 600 enormous stone statues of men wearing hats like crowns. Some of these statues are about 30 feet tall. Nobody really knows why they were made, but perhaps they are images of kings or gods. The craft workers who made them used logs of wood as rollers and levers to move them into place.

BELIEFS AND IDEAS

Today people believe in the power of human beings to change the world through science, politics, or war. These ideas would have shocked the people living in Marco Polo's time. They believed that God or unseen spirits controlled people's lives. God or spirits made people sick, healed them, brought rain, or caused famine. Floods, droughts, and earthquakes were often seen as punishments for people's sins. In many countries only one religion was allowed, and rulers punished anyone who broke religious laws.

▲ A statue of a Zen holy figure meditating. Zen teachers asked people to show their faith by meditation and hard work.

ZEN BUDDHISM

EAST ASIA

In China and Japan many people were Buddhists. They followed the teachings of Buddha, a religious thinker who lived around 550 B.C. He taught his followers that they must learn to control their thoughts and actions and live good lives. This was more important than worshiping gods. One form of Buddhism, known as Zen, was popular among samurai warriors in Japan in Marco Polo's time. Helped by Zen meditation, samurai warriors followed a strict code of honor called Bushido. They believed that it was nobler to die fighting bravely in battle than to suffer defeat.

► The fourteenth-century mosque at Jenné, Mali, is built of clay and timber in the traditional African style.

◄ A Chinese family offer food and drink to the spirits of their dead ancestors.

FAMILY LIFE

Many Chinese people followed the teachings of Confucius, a scholar who lived around 500 B.C. He believed that people should respect the law and uphold traditional family values. Families, like the one pictured above, also believed their dead ancestors could protect and help them.

FIRE, WIND, AND WATER

Mongols worshipped Tengri, god of heaven, and Itugan, goddess of earth. They believed that all living things had spirits, and that fire, water, and the winds were sacred, too. Unlike other Mongol rulers, Kublai Khan was interested in many different faiths. He invited religious leaders from distant lands to visit him at his court.

► This soapstone bird sculpture comes from Zimbabwe. It shows an eagle-spirit, which carries messages between people and gods.

MANY GODS

SOUTH ASIA

Worshipers at Hindu temples said prayers to many different gods in human or animal shape, such as the elephant-headed god Ganesha (see page 37). Each of these gods looked after one part of human life, such as trade, childbirth, or war.

ISLAMIC FAITH

AFRICA

In North Africa many people followed the faith of Islam. Worshipers prayed and listened to preachers in splendid mosques. In universities, scholars studied religious texts and Muslim laws. In Marco Polo's time, traders helped to spread the Islamic faith to countries farther south.

NATURE SPIRITS

South of the Sahara many people followed ancient traditional beliefs. They worshiped nature spirits, which lived in holy places such as mountains or rivers, or in wild creatures. They also honored dead ancestors and living kings. African priests held ceremonies with dancing and chanting to heal people, bring victory, or make rain.

HOME OF ISLAM

Muslims from many lands went on pilgrimages to the holy city of Mecca, in Arabia. This was where the Prophet Muhammad first received revelations from God. They were later written down in a holy book called the Qur'an. Muslims believe it contains a message from God, telling people the right way to live. Christians and Jews also lived in the Middle East. They were protected by Muslim law but had to pay extra taxes. They were better treated than minority groups in many European countries.

▼ A painting of St. Francis of Assisi. In the thirteenth century, he set up a group of wandering preachers, called friars, which means "brothers."

EAST AND WEST

In western Europe, Christians belonged to the Roman Catholic Church, led by the Pope. In eastern Europe they belonged to the Orthodox Church, led by the Patriarch. In Marco Polo's time Church leaders had their own armies and often quarreled with kings. Many Christians made pilgrimages to pray at sacred shrines. Here they could see the relics of saints and special religious paintings called icons. They believed that relics and icons had miraculous powers to answer prayers.

MONKS, NUNS, AND FRIARS

In Europe there were groups of religious men and women called monks and nuns. They lived apart from the everyday world and devoted their lives to God. They gave up all possessions and promised not to marry. They spent their time studying, working, and praying. Some monks and nuns worked as teachers or ran hospitals. Groups of preachers called friars wandered around the countryside, telling ordinary people about God.

◄ This thirteenth-century icon (religious painting) comes from Moscow. Icons were painted only for the Orthodox Church.

◄ A medicine bundle from the Crow people of North America. Bundles like this contained natural objects, such as feathers or stones. They were collected by people at special moments in their lives. Some people thought that they had magical powers.

RAIN AND TEARS

AMERICAS

Each Native American group in North and South America worshiped in its own special ways. But their religions had one thing in common: They respected the living world. They held special ceremonies at important times in the year, such as first rains and harvest, to encourage crops to grow or to make buffalo herds increase. The ceremonies of some groups involved suffering or human sacrifices. These people believed that by offering pain or blood to nature spirits, they helped the world to continue. In Mexico the Aztecs believed that babies' tears would bring life-giving rain. In North America, warriors danced around and around, tearing at their flesh, to make the sun shine on their fields and farms.

▼ This massive rock, called Uluru, is an ancient holy site in Australia. It is still a holy place for Aboriginal peoples.

LUCKY CHARMS

AUSTRALASIA

In Australia and the islands of the Pacific, people believed that certain places were specially holy. Worshipers could feel close to nature spirits there, or contact long-dead ancestors, who gave strength to people still alive.

In Australia, Aborigines danced and played music at holy sites, recreating the Dreamtime, a magical era long ago. In Polynesia, worshipers made offerings in front of statues of gods, asking for help and protection from volcanoes, dangerous animals, and storms at sea. They also trusted in magical carvings called tikis, which could carry a curse or a lucky charm.

PEOPLES FROM AROUND THE WORLD

GLOSSARY

Aborigines The first inhabitants of Australia, who arrived there about 40,000 years ago.

Anasazi A Native American group that lived in hot, dry regions of southwest North America, between about A.D.100 and 1300.

Aztec A civilization in Central Mexico, powerful from about A.D. 1300–1520.

Chimu A civilization in Peru, in South America, gradually taken over by the Incas about A.D.1300.

Hopi Native Americans from the semidesert regions of southwest North America. Some of their pueblo sites have been occupied continuously for about 1,000 years.

Inca A civilization in Peru and neighboring lands in South America, powerful from about A.D. 1200–1530.

Inuit Native Americans who arrived in the Arctic regions of North America about 2000 B.C.

Maoris Settlers in New Zealand who came from Pacific Islands from about A.D. 800.

Maya A civilization in southern Mexico, most powerful from about A.D. 250–900. But many of their beliefs and traditions survived to influence the Toltec and Aztec civilizations.

Mongols Nomads who originally lived on the wide grassy plains north of China. Around 1200 they began to move south and west, forming a vast empire.

Native Americans The first inhabitants of America, who arrived there about 30,000 years ago. Native American people were divided into more than 200 different groups, with different languages and lifestyles.

Pacific peoples/Polynesians People who lived on islands in the Pacific Ocean. They were descended from settlers who migrated there from South and East Asia.

Shona A people living in southeast Africa. The Shona people built the city of Great Zimbabwe about A.D. 1250.

Thule A civilization that spread from Greenland across the Arctic regions of North America from about A.D. 1000.

Toltec A civilization in Mexico, powerful from about A.D. 900–1220. The Toltecs were excellent builders and craft workers.

Afghan A person from Afghanistan, a country in Central Asia.
ancestor: A long-dead relative.
Angkor A city in Cambodia, home of the Khmer emperors, who ruled a powerful empire in Southeast Asia from A.D. 800-1300.
architect Someone who designs buildings.
the arts Music, art, and literature.
astronomer A scientist who studies the stars and planets.

barter To trade goods for other goods, rather than money.
bazaar A market, especially in North Africa, Asia, or the Middle East.
booming Describes trade that is very successful.
Buddha A name for Siddhartha Gautama, a prince who lived in India in the sixth century B.C. He founded the religion of **Buddhism**, teaching his followers to seek truth and the right way to live through meditation.

casting Making an object or figure by pouring liquid metal or glass into a shaped mold.
Church Refers to the organization of the Christian religion, rather than to the building where Christians worship.
civilization A society with its own laws, customs, beliefs, and artistic traditions.
codex An Aztec book written in pictures, telling the histories of people and gods.

commission To order and pay for a project to be carried out.
coral A hard, often beautifully colored material formed by the skeletons of tiny sea animals.

drawbridge A bridge that can be raised to keep people out.
Dreamtime The name given by the Aboriginal people of Australia to the beginning of the world, when spirits created earth and sky.
dye A mixture of earth, plants, metals, and, nowadays, chemicals, used to color things.
dynasty A series of rulers belonging to the same family.

environment The surroundings in which people, plants, and animals live.
exotic Strange and unusual, coming from a distant land.

Far East A name sometimes used to describe the countries of East Asia, including China and Japan.
felt Thick cloth made by pressing and boiling wool.
fire To bake at a high temperature to harden clay or to melt a glaze.

geometric Describes designs that are based on circles, triangles, and other simple shapes.
glaze A smooth, glassy coating, used to waterproof clay objects and make them more beautiful.
gold leaf Gold that has been hammered to a thin sheet.
gothic A style of art and architecture fashionable between about A.D. 1100 and 1500. Gothic buildings have tall doors and windows and pointed arches.
governor The ruler of a region that is part of a country or empire.

Hindu A person who follows the Hindu religion, which grew up in India between about 1500–600 B.C. Hindus worship many gods, but they are all forms of one supreme god, Brahma.
Holy Land The city of Jerusalem and the surrounding land.

import To buy or bring in goods from another country.
irrigate To channel water into dry land, so crops can grow there.
Islam The worship of Allah (God), taught by Muhammad, a prophet who lived in Arabia from A.D. 570–632. Followers of Islam are called **Muslims**.
ivory The hard substance that elephant's tusks are made of.

kiwi A flightless bird that lives in New Zealand.

magnetic compass An instrument for finding direction. It has a magnetic needle that always points north.
medieval Of the period of time from around A.D. 500–1500, also called the Middle Ages.
meditation Thinking deeply about spiritual things.
memorial A building or object made in honor of a dead person or past event.
merchant A person who buys and sells goods.
Middle East A term used to describe countries on the eastern shores of the Mediterranean Sea, plus Turkey, Arabia, Iran, and Iraq.
millet A cereal grass like wheat.
minority group A group of people within a larger population whose beliefs, traditions, or origins are different from the rest.

mosque A building where Muslims pray and study.
mother-of-pearl A hard, shiny substance found inside some shells.
multicultural Describes a society where people from different ethnic groups live side by side.
Muslim See Islam.

nomad A person who moves from place to place in search of food and water.

peace treaty An agreement made between rulers to end war.
pilgrim A person who makes a special journey called a **pilgrimage** to visit a holy place.
Pope The head of the Roman Catholic Church, based in Rome.
porcelain A kind of fine china.
portcullis A frame of iron or wooden bars set into a gateway, which can be raised or lowered.

relics The remains of (or object associated with) a holy person, kept as a memorial.
revelation God's showing himself or his wishes to people.

sacrifice The killing of a person or animal to please the gods.
scholarship Study and learning.
scribe A specially trained person who kept written records or copied books by hand.
soapstone A soft stone that is easy to carve.

tax To demand official payment of money, goods, or service.

warlord A warrior leader, who had control over parts of a country.

yam A kind of root vegetable.

INDEX